This book belongs to:

....

....

Preface

This story was written to provide an historic awareness and knowledge of African-American history for children.
The events as
described by the characters are real; with some fictitious character involvement. This story is meant to provoke and promote pride, identity, respect and greatness in the reader. The ultimate goal of this book is to help children honor and embrace the strength of their elders and ancestors while connecting with the richness of their own flow of royalty.

May they never limit themselves because they will see the garment of greatness in the tapestry of their own lives because of
what was… and IS!
Nettie, Nana, and Friends Educational Puppeteering Company LLC
www.nettieandnana.com
nettieandnana@gmail.com

Nettie, Nana & Friends
Education. Puppeteering. Purpose!

Nettie, Nana & Friends
Education. Puppeteering. Purpose!

Dedications

This book is dedicated to the heroes of African-American history! To the families of those whose sacrifice transcends time. To the unsung heroes, never mentioned or written about, I dedicate this book to you! To our beautiful children all over the world, of every race, culture, and ethnicity, may you find that YOU are the world's GREATEST ASSET! History is written each day you breathe. Know that YOU are the changemakers who carry the trophy for all those who came before! Love, Respect, and Care for your elders as they have cared for YOU! We dedicate this book to you.

Remember: You can do ALL things through Christ who strengthens you.
KJV: Phillians 4:13
God bless,
Ronnette Smith-Powell and Destiny Powell

Colorful streamers sparkled. The sound of chatter filled the halls of Sunville Elementary School. It was the week before the Big Multicultural Celebration.

Ms. Cooper reminded the students to dress up as a hero from their cultural background. Corey was excited because he already knew who he was going to be!

Multicultural Day is coming!

Guion Bluford

Corey ran into the living room like a bolt of lightning. "Nana...Nana," he yelled. "Can you take me to Shopmart, pleeease!? I'm going to soar into space like GUION BLUFORD, the FIRST BLACK ASTRONAUT!"

"Oh, I don't know about that, Sweet Potato. My arthritis is acting up something awful today."

"Who's Arthur Itis?" Corey inquired.

"Oh, my goodness," Nana replied. "Let me explain."

"I have arthritis, my dear. That means my joints get stiff. Sometimes it hurts to bend or move around."

Corey listened...and wanted to help!

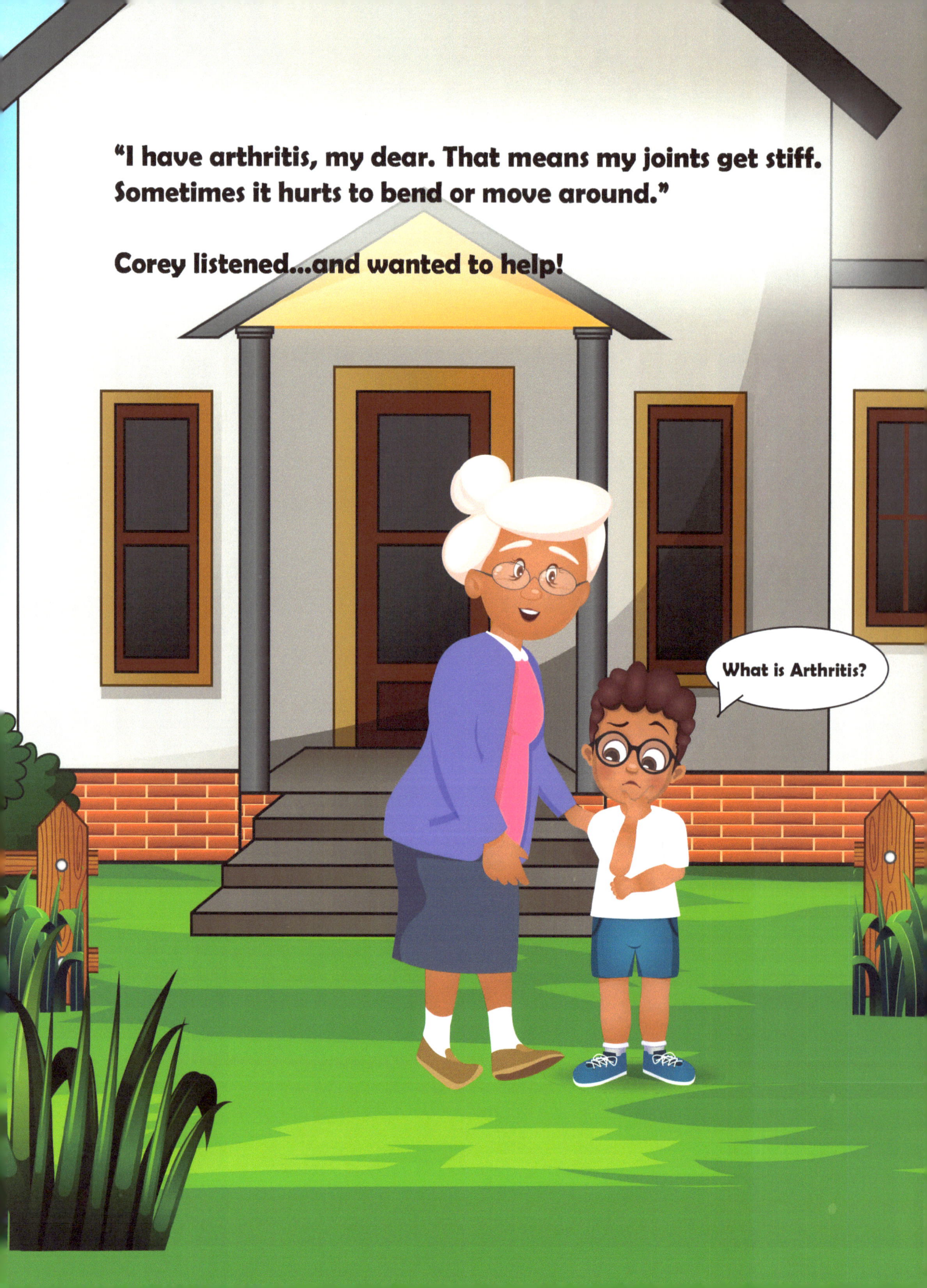

What is Arthritis?

"You see, I need a little more time to do the things that you can do easily. That's why I use a cane to help me steady myself."

With a soft whimper, Corey asked, "Why do you have arthritis, Nana?"

"Nana is 92, my darling. My heart has been beating a long time. These ol' eyes have seen a whole lot of things. Come here, Sweet Potato."

I love you Nana

Corey and Nana sat on the sofa. Nana slowly bent down to a small space below the bookcase and pulled out an old and tattered photo album. Nana began sharing.

What's that!?

"You see, this is me back in 1963. I marched on Washington with the great Dr. Martin Luther King Jr. He was a powerful Baptist minister and social activist who led the civil rights movement."

Corey's eyes widened. He had never seen Nana with black hair.

Rosa Parks

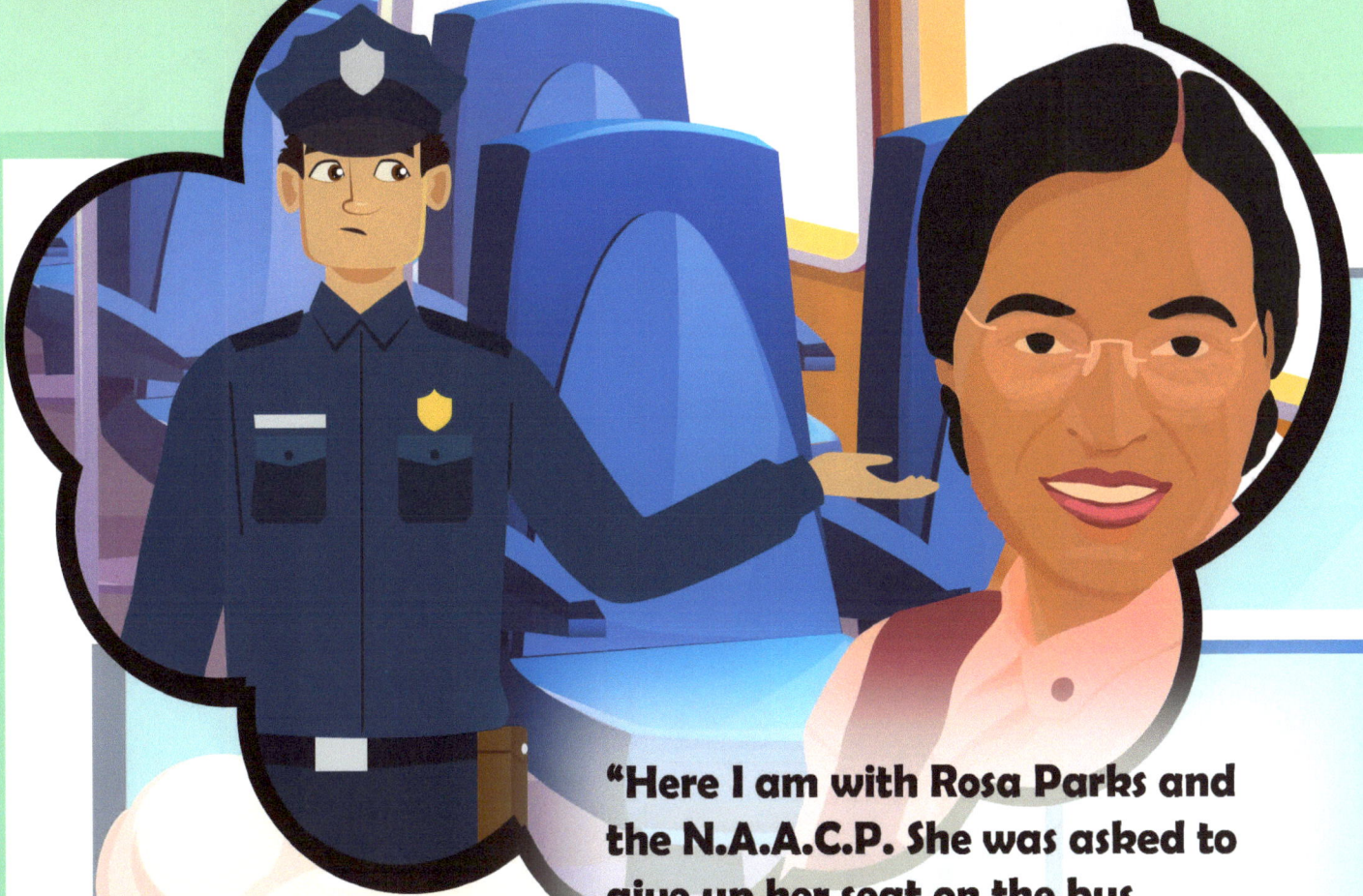

"Here I am with Rosa Parks and the N.A.A.C.P. She was asked to give up her seat on the bus because of the color of her skin. ROSA refused, and was thrown in jail. So WE had to BOYCOTT!"

Corey imagined how he would've felt if he was forced to give up his seat on the school bus because of his smooth brown skin.
His eyes narrowed!

N.A.A.C.P

"What does N.A.A.C.P mean?" Corey asked.

"Those letters stand for: The National Association for the Advancement of Colored People. We are America's oldest and largest civil rights organization."

Corey had even more questions. "What are Civil Rights?" Nana explained, "ALL People are created equally. Civil Rights means EVERYONE has the right to freedom and fairness. Black, White, Hispanic, Haitian or any other nationality, we are all God's beautiful handywork."

Corey leaned in so close that their arms met like cornbread and butter!

Thurgood Marshall

"Do you know who this is?" Nana asked.
Corey stared long and hard at the photo.
Papa interrupted...
"That's me and Thurgood Marshall, the Supreme Court's first African American justice," Papa said, as he walked into the room.

"Wow," said Corey, handing Nana a glass of water to take her pain medicine.

Shirley Chisholm

"Oh, and this picture right here is my friend Shirley Chisholm," Nana said. "She was the First African American woman to serve in Congress in 1968 and she was the first WOMAN to seek the presidential nomination...mmm hum!"

Corey couldn't believe his ears!

Harriet Tubman

"You see that little girl in this picture, Corey? THAT'S ME with your great-grandparents. Did you know that Harriet Tubman helped them find their way to freedom from Maryland to Philadelphia on the secret Underground Railroad?"

"They had trains back then, Nana?" Corey asked. Nana smiled as she explained. "The Underground Railroad was a secret path from the South to the North that Harriet used to help the enslaved escape to freedom."

Jackie Robinson

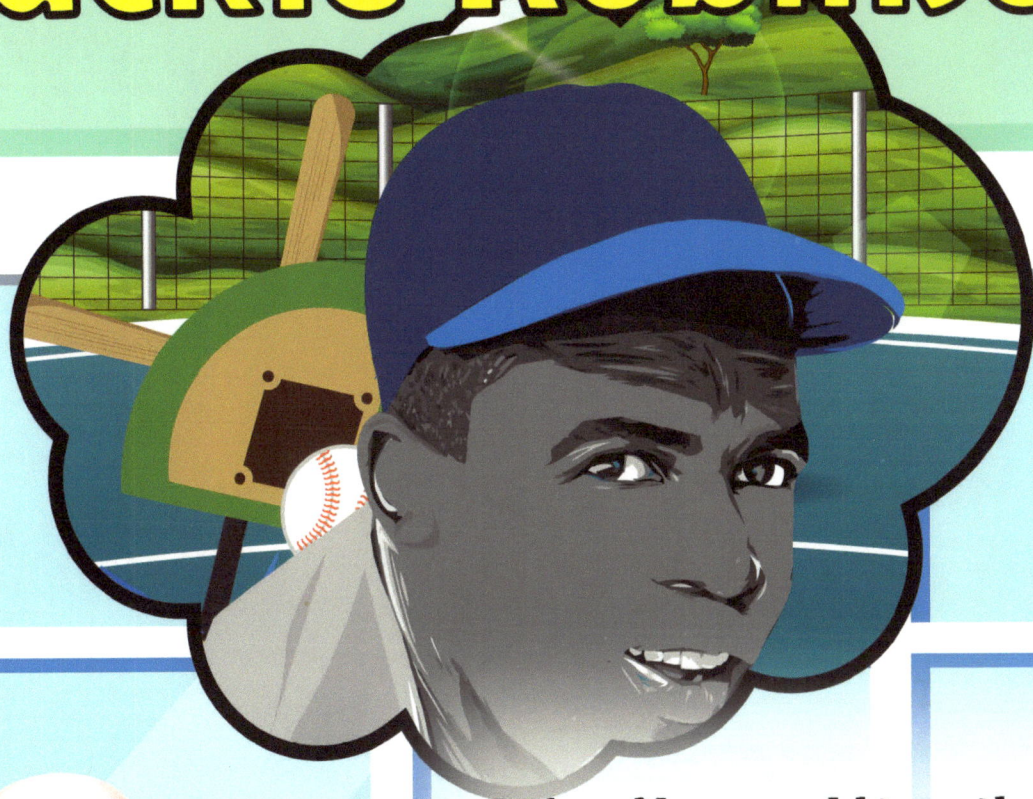

Before Nana could turn the page, Corey had already begun to ask... "Is that my Uncle Theadore?" "Oh my, Corey, you have the eyes of an eagle. Yes, it is. He's at the baseball game with the great Jackie Robinson, the first African American to play in the major leagues."

Corey loved playing baseball with his friends Juan, Ahmed, Tom, Michael, and the rest of the team. He was so glad that Jackie Robinson paved the way to end segregation. Now everyone can play together!

Barack Obama

Papa continued, "Here you are as a little baby."
Corey looked closely.
"We are in Washington D.C. celebrating the inauguration of the FIRST AFRICAN AMERICAN PRESIDENT, Barack Obama! That's his lovely wife Michelle Obama and their two beautiful daughters."

"My dear Corey," Nana went on, "We have ALWAYS been kings and queens. Greatness and Royalty are in our blood. From the great plains of AFRICA to the alleys of America, there is NOTHING we as a people cannot do! You don't need to ask permission to BE GREAT because YOU already ARE!"

Guion Bluford.

Nana slowly pushed her glasses up on her nose as she turned the page to a yellow-stained newspaper clipping. Corey squealed with delight... "Guion Bluford!!"
"Yes, Sweet Potato! That's 'Guy,'" Nana said laughing. "We always called him that! WE were so proud to see him launch into space on the Challenger in 1983."

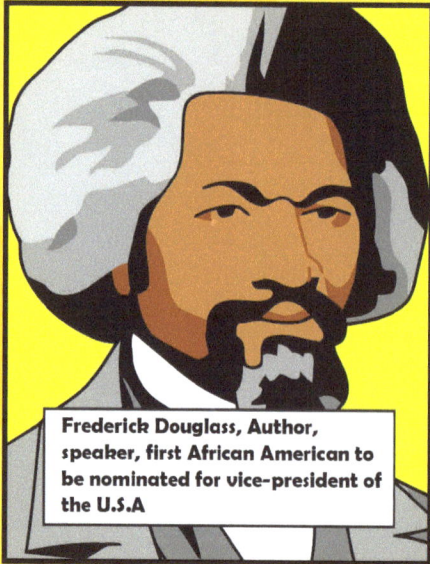

Frederick Douglass, Author, speaker, first African American to be nominated for vice-president of the U.S.A

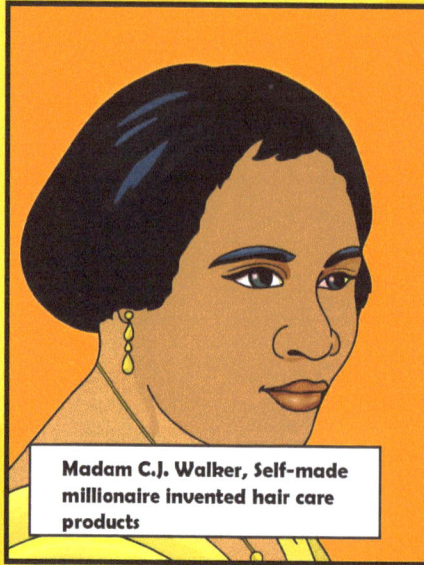

Madam C.J. Walker, Self-made millionaire invented hair care products

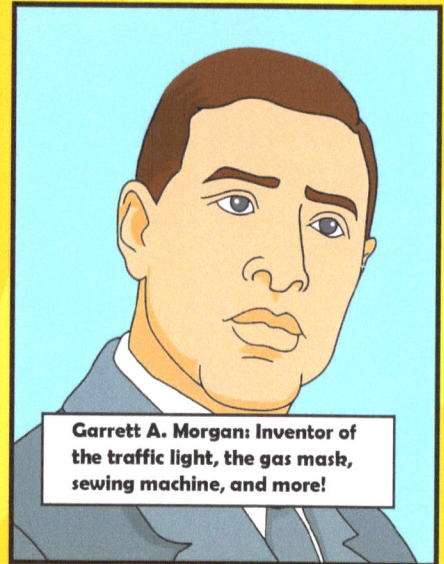

Garrett A. Morgan: Inventor of the traffic light, the gas mask, sewing machine, and more!

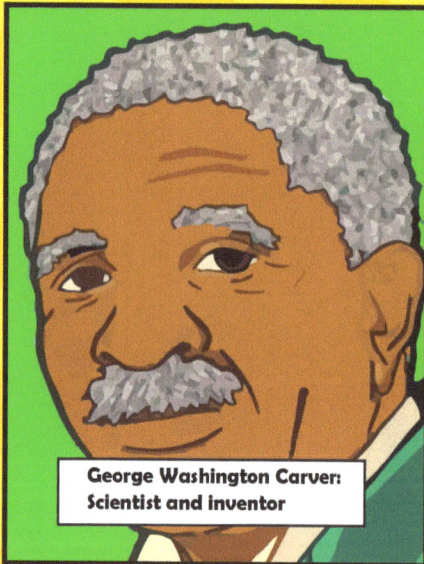

George Washington Carver: Scientist and inventor

Maya Angelou: Poet and civil rights activist

Nana shared more photos, including Frederick Douglass, Madam C.J. Walker, Garret A. Morgan, George Washington Carver, and many more amazing African Americans.

Corey's face beamed with pride as he gently rubbed a dab of mint-smelling arthritis cream on Nana's hands! "You sure have done and seen a lot, Nana!"

"That's right, my dear! That's why you must always RESPECT your elders. We have fought long and hard so YOU all will HAVE a BETTER PATH to travel."

"I know what that means, Nana!"
Nana's face began to glow like the sun.
"Respect means to honor, admire and treat with kindness and care!"
"That's right, Sweet Potato!"

Corey wrapped a soft yellow sweater around Nana as she continued. "You see, Corey, I haven't always been a senior! My arms and legs have fought and marched and helped to win many battles. Arthritis might hurt my joints but it can't stop my heart from loving you."

Corey Listened...Corey Knew he was strong, he was Brave, and he was GREAT!

Corey ran to his closet to get his red and gold Dashiki!
"That's my boy," Nana sang out as he strutted into the living room.
"That garment is the fabric of pride. It connects us with our homeland and culture of Africa!"

Corey slowly helped Nana off the sofa. He looked closely at Nana's soft wrinkled hands. He listened as her joints creaked when she adjusted her weight on the walker. He studied how her feet shuffled like sandpaper across the floor.

He thought about all the wonderful people in the album. He would've been proud to be any of them for Multicultural Day!

Corey was ready to soar to the moon just like Guion Bluford--not just because he loved the stars and the galaxy but because the sky had no limit to what he could do!

Corey realized that HE too would one day have stories to tell of how magnificent and awesome his grandmother IS and will ALWAYS BE!

Corey's eyes looked around the table at each member of his family. He suddenly understood that it was HIS turn to CARE for NANA as she, his family, and his ancestors had cared for him.

Corey knew Greatness and Royalty were in him and he could do ANYTHING he set his mind to just like YOU!

Glossary

Multicultural: people of various groups or cultures, nations, or traditions.

Civil Rights: fair, equal treatment of all people.

Arthritis: swelling, inflammation, or pain in the joints between the bones, making it hard to move.

N.A.A.C.P: (National Association for the Advancement of Colored People) a civil rights activist group that protects and promotes fair and equal treatment of African Americans.

Congress: the part of the government that makes the laws for the country. Congress is made up of the US Senate and the House of Representatives.

Underground Railroad: escape route for enslaved people.

Segregation: to keep apart or separate.

Ancestor(s): part of a family that has passed away. (Example: The Elders, forefathers, great-grandparents, etc.)

Discussion Questions:

1. If your school had a Multicultural Day, who would you want to be for the celebration?

2. What did you like most about this story?

3. What were some ways Corey showed respect for his Nana?

4. How can you show RESPECT to your family members for the things they have done for you?

Meet the Authors

Ronnette Smith-Powell a proud wife, mother, entrepreneur, author, puppeteer, performer, mentor, vocalist, motivational speaker, educator and CEO,. She has enjoyed teaching for over twenty-five years. She began her career teaching first and second grade in the city of Newark, NJ, where she was born and grew up. Presently, she passionately teaches kindergarten in Willingboro, NJ. In 1995, Ronnette earned a Bachelor of Arts degree in Elementary Education from Kean University, and in 2013, she continued on with a Master of Education degree in Curriculum and Instruction in Reading with an Emphasis in Elementary Education from Grand Canyon University.

Destiny Powell (Ronnette's daughter/co-author/business partner) is a seventh-grade honor student who loves to express herself through performing arts and writing. Her parents work together to cultivate her aspirations. Creativity flows through this dynamic duo's innovative books and puppeteering and performing arts company!

Nettie, Nana, and Friends, LLC. This dynamic team works together to create an educational platform with passion and purpose! Its electrifying and interactive performances include motivational leadership training, student puppeteering workshops, interactive read-alouds, and puppet shows on character education, social-emotional wellness, biblical principles, African American studies, health and safety,
multicultural awareness, and more!
Ronnette's love for children and her ability to give them a voice, together with Destiny's creativity have inspired these great titles. Look for more great titles by this dedicated and inspiring team of new authors!

- They have appeared on NBC10 News, Good Morning Philadelphia, and FOX29!
- Received a personal phone call from New Jersey's Governor Phil Murphy.
- Awarded a Certificate of Congressional Recognition from Congressman Andy Kim.
- In the NJEA Dec. 2021 issue of Review Magazine
- Supported by Acenda Health, South New Jersey Perinatal Cooperative, Sisterhood/Covid-Con,
- Performed Educational Puppet shows for NAACP, Schools, Daycares, Libraries, Community Events, Churches, and more!

Follow this amazing team of authors! Visit www.nettieandnana.com for more information!

Highlight Moments